Wisdom Tree of Life

Put God First

Tony Aldana

Copyrights © 2025. Tony Aldana. All Rights Reserved.

No part of this book may be reproduced, distributed, or transmitted in any form or by any means, including photocopying, recording, or other electronic or mechanical methods, without the prior written permission of the publisher, except in the case of brief quotations used for review purposes.

Dedication

This book is dedicated to the communities from the ghetto to the suburbs. Much love and respect to the whole city of Houston, TX, Vero "Conchita," Lil Eastside, Chikis, Black, and Jorge. A Sanchez, Grandpa Don Lupe, Grandma Doña Guicha, Chicha, and all the rest of the family members.

Words can't explain how I feel, so I'm showing you by writing this book. My family is too big to name everybody, but it's self-explanatory.

Acknowledgments

I'm highly grateful and feel blessed to have GOD, my family, as a senior project coordinator in KDP BOOK PUBLISHING and **Imaad Ismail**, a mentor to all my questions. I appreciate the Houston streets for modeling me into who I am today. I survived the best and the worst, good and bad, but I never folded, so I always stayed above water.

About the Author

I faced every obstacle with my head up and chest out, from life and death experiences to reliable acknowledgment from within. I'm addicted to strategizing my objectives for self-accomplishment—a successful completion from me and others. Never let your past define you through other people's eyes.

Table of Contents

Wisdom Tree of Life: Put God First i
Introduction 1
Chapter 1 8
Chapter 2 16
Chapter 3 23
Chapter 4 29
Chapter 5 36
Chapter 6 42
Chapter 7 48
Chapter 8 53
Chapter 9 59
Chapter 10 64

Wisdom Tree of Life

Put God First

Introduction

The cover has $100 bills with the blue holographic strip, $50, $20, $10, $5, $1, and $2 bills as substitutes for leaves on the branches. Money is made of paper. Paper is made from a tree, so money does grow on trees. I have platinum and gold apples representing our minds as victorious conquers in the puzzle to see the bigger picture. You allow me to plant positive seeds in your mind by reading my book. Keep analyzing positive information; that's how you water seeds, growing them into completion. You see different roots under the tree because it's true we come from different roots but are all connected to the same tree, the tree of life. We all consume food and drink water the same way. We urinate and defecate no different. We breathe the same. Our bodies bleed and heal only one way by a scab or scar. Nobody lives forever, only spiritually through GOD eternally.

Eventually, the flesh expires in due time, so live life to the fullest. I got tired of using people only to satisfy myself. It was time to give back constructively to all the people I hurt physically, mentally, and spiritually. Releasing venom when your mind absorbs poison is negative for the community because many residents will get injured by the destruction of selfish actions. My main concentration is on the ghetto children, unseasoned minors, and young adults. But if I can reach grown people, that would also be a plus. I know I won't be able to change the world's perspective. As long as I touch one child and one adult, I'm satisfied because it's a domino effect after the positive seed's been successfully planted.

These children are the future. If they grow up misled, guess what? Our future is tampered with corruption and hopelessness.

This book is for the targets of manipulation, hypnotized, cursed, and possessed by their street life demons. I know because I used to be fighting them until I found GOD, and GOD found me. That life is not so glamorous but more devilish a promoter for evil. All they see is the material possessions received from fast money, which triggers an illusion of lust, a never-ending cycle of failure. Nobody tells them the other part when they are locked up, taken away from their loved ones, lied to, witnessed betrayal, robbed, or killed by the same people inside their same group, all for the love of fast money. If they have kids, they leave the children to be raised by strangers. We, the people, need to stop judging each other by whose race is more intelligent, dominant, or financially stable instead of bringing each other down. We need to build each other up, not make fun of someone when they have made a mistake, and help them become better decision-makers. If you know the answer they are searching for, assist them in a way that they keep studying for more. We, the people, need to realize that two minds are stronger than one. The more, the better. In order to be labeled a boss, you have to have a master mind team. Working together to accomplish desired goals. They stay in control by separating us. Separation unfolds from confinement. Just like uniting us together as one, we form an unstoppable, potent force. The fastest way they stay in control is by instilling fear in us through the internet, media, television, radio, or newspapers. We, the people, need to stop setting limitations on ourselves and others. The sky is the limit; we were born to shine like a bag full of diamonds. We, the people, need to learn how to look at every obstacle by anything and every obstacle as a blessing.

The younger generation is easily influenced by anything and everything because all the O.G.'s "teachers" are either dead or locked up for a long time. So, they feel that since most of them are gone for a while, it's closed ears to good advice. It's the blind leading the blind. In order to be a teacher, you have to be a leader; in order to be a leader, you have to be a teacher. Every teacher was a student at one time. Don't feel ashamed, discouraged, or belittled yourself only because you were born with less than the rest. Even though we are in a mess, we are still blessed. Our minds are like sponges. Everything we soak up has to get released from the inside out. Positive thoughts embrace positive results and vice versa with the negative. Do you know what's more powerful than a nuclear weapon, rifle, or gun? It's the mind, so feed it fruitful thoughts to keep a healthy thinking process, cluster it with junk, and your temple will crumble in due time. If someone makes you believe you're getting sick, manifest it mentally, and you will become physically sick. You are who you associate with. Piggish ways will have you moving slimy. It's the law of attraction. To run circles around someone is to outsmart someone. The image is standing still, and another person is running around him at 200 mph before they realize what's going on. It's possible to fall under somebody's command without them having to point a gun. People disguise their true emotions like a costume, so you can't see their true intentions behind the smoke screen.

I'm here to expose the foolishness and help the blind see vision by removing the blindfold before they crash into a brick wall. Dear heavenly Father from the heavens above, I want to thank you for waking me up to see another blessed day. I am a living witness to your miracles. Use me to guide them to the light. They have been trapped in the dark. Allow me to be there for them through this book from the cradle to the grave.

Tony Aldana

Chapter 1

Pick your head up; you're the chosen one, the one that swam harder and faster than the rest of the seeds of semen. As soon as we were brought into this world, the doctors let our parents cherish this special moment to enjoy for themselves for bringing a beautiful newborn child into this world. Then they take us away for medical reasons. When it's time for our people to come see us, we're peacefully asleep amongst other newborns, but wait!!!

We just took our first official breath after being in the womb. So, we are full of life, screaming, crying, swinging, and kicking; this is the only way we can communicate at this time. But now we are in a coma, snoozing deeply asleep. So, I wonder what they really injected us with? We were born into this world innocent. From crawling to walking, every step is calculated. We mocked and imitated everything we saw and heard. Babies are not born with hatred or are known to have a sexual orientation of the same sex. The one and only creator will punish tampering with the innocent in due time of judgment. Children can be the reflections of their parents or the reflections of the environments surrounding them.

Deluded conversations with hidden agendas behind the deals and agreements for sale. It was manipulation at its finest. To this day, Indians still receive checks. The schools in low-income neighborhoods will only teach them so much. The schools in the upper-class neighborhood will teach them how to prosper in life, how to start a business, and how to run a business successfully. A method made to keep the poor, poor, and the rich wealthy by dividing us up, keeping a balance between the people only if you accept their program. Everybody can't stays poor, just like everybody can't becomes rich.

We were all born with platinum and gold minds, but they want us to think it's copper or brass. Never stop wanting to learn more; procrastination is the downfall for 80% of the population, ain't no rewards ever handed out to laziness. Thomas Edison was an American inventor who invented the microphone in 1877, the phonograph in 1878, the incandescent lamp in 1879, and even installed the world's first central electric power plant in New York City in 1882. He received more than a thousand bad bits of advice before he invented the light, like stop already, you're wasting your time, just give up already, it will never work, and to this day, we still use the light. They wouldn't say anything if you weren't doing anything right.

Hatred and jealousy are germs that can turn into diseases. It's highly contagious. Stay away from people who practice these toxic emotions into mastery. It's a virus that infects humans who don't like watching others achieve success. Don't listen to the twisted whispers of the devil. His words cause harm and destruction. Rotten thoughts evolve into evil voices. Thinking negatively will trick the mind into being negative; it's all in your head. Don't drive your own self crazy. Feed the mind with fruitful thoughts so it can process healthy thinking. Visualize yourself accomplishing desired goals. After finishing one, set another goal. Never stay content in the position you're in. Good or bad consultation should be examined for better results in future situations. Learn how to filter out stupidity and valuable information to edify your next moves. Leave the past as the past; don't let it define you. It only molds you into a more competent decision-making person. Why would you keep looking back if you're trying to move forward?

Eventually, you would crash against a brick wall. If the road you're driving on is rocky, why not choose smoother pavement to glide on?

The highway of riches is the only freeway worth riding on, sliding through the interstate. Everything else is irrelevant; never exit your destination; it should be endless. I look at every downfall and setback as a blessing. Even when I came to prison, I found myself putting God first.

Only the Lord knows if I would still be in those streets. I would have gotten killed or killed someone, and my stay in prison would have been way longer, with no re-entry back into society. I had to ask myself why I was coming home, might as well stay locked up if all I'm going to do is hurt my family and myself by returning to prison.

Change is good; don't be intimidated by doing something different from others.

Unless you want to keep dragging your body through the ground, it's the law of life. Even the caterpillar graduated. It transforms into a butterfly; staying on the ground is only temporary. We have to isolate ourselves like a cocoon, then spread our wings and fly. Explore life for greater conditions with better opportunities. Time waits for no man. To become a winner, you have to get tired of losing.

The struggle comes first before you shine. You learn how to value your success more when you earn it. Instead of someone who has been pampered their entire life and handed down currency by the bundles, they will eventually lose everything faster than the speed of lightning. When you worked for it, you understand better on how to build an empire and what it took to form the foundation.

Adults don't need others to hold their hands to walk across the street. Some people can't think past the present. It doesn't mean they're useless because when you play chess, each piece is useful. Use people in a good way for good reasons. Don't mistreat people. Using people for the wrong motives will only backfire. It's best to have everybody on the same page, working in harmony as one. A boss will make sure everybody eats. So they can feed their own family outside the mastermind team.

Everybody has different positions to fill. Treat every team member equally with respect so they won't builds up animosity toward each other. The person giving instructions shouldn't play the favoritism game. Remember, it's chess, not checkers. When greeting in a handshake, ensure you have a firm grip because a weak, delicate handshake says a lot about a person. A company will only succeed through everybody's cooperation.

Chapter 2

I was helping people when I didn't even know how to help myself. Before my uncles taught me how to swim, my mom used to sit me on the little kid's side of the pool, where I would chill by the steps. There was a little girl sitting next to me. Her commotion of drowning, trying to stay above water, grabbed my attention after I observed her for a couple of seconds. Trying to figure out what I'm looking at. It was like my sixth sense kicked in and told me to help her. After I picked her up, the grown-ups ran over to our location to witness her throw up water. I picked her up right on time, and she didn't even have to go to the hospital.

I believe in infinite intelligence from a higher power outside of the sources of one's own mind. Informational plans floating around in the air are how we embrace some new ideas out of the blue. Have you ever had a problem trying to figure out the solution? But your mind seems cloudy, burned out. Let your brain rest from thinking so much and sleep on it. When you wake up, your brain will automatically come up with the answer.

Do you know what is more powerful than a nuclear weapon, rifle, or gun?

It's the mind, but almost everybody doesn't like using it. They would rather have technology do everything for them. Some would rather let a computer think for them. Show them how to comprehend, and ask them questions about life. Most people never accomplish anything because they are not sure what they want to do in life. They want to be presidents or doctors one day, and the next day, they finish watching a new movie or reading an urban book. Now, they kingpin drug dealers.

Don't get my words twisted; I call it how I see it. I'm not a promoter for wrongdoers, but the truth is, if El Chapo and Pablo Escobar couldn't do it, what makes you think that you can do it better? It's a fantasy they painted in their own minds. There's no future in selling drugs on my behalf. Tell me who loves to watch their backs 24/7. If the closest ones on your own squad don't cross you, people envy you. They'll try hard to leave you in the grave or want you in prison with a life sentence for protecting what's yours.

And your children who get left behind are the real victims. But supposedly, the hustle was to provide for them; now you're locked up; who's providing for them since you're no longer in the picture? Ain't no telling. It's a cold world, especially if you're a little girl or boy who doesn't have a father figure to protect them or guide them in a righteous way.

It's rare to find an individual who treats your child with the same love and affection as he does his own child that he had with your baby's mother.

So, think twice when you see drug dealers flashing a lot of money, driving fancy cars, living in big houses, and with females in flocks. That happiness is only temporary, that feeling, that feeling is not real, it's only for the moment. Everybody's smiling for the wrong reasons.

Once in the grave, you're forgotten like you never did anything for them, or when you're locked up, your worst enemies or best friend sleeps with your wife.

The ones you think are down for life never write, visit, or send money. But these are the same people you used to pay for everything, living lavishly, right?

They didn't need anything, but you were hustling for something, a purpose, right? Perpetrating an unattainable image is nonsense. An ashtray easily influences clueless marbles.

Everything materialistic is replaceable, and as soon as you get it, it is as fast as you can lose it. As soon as you lose it, it is as fast as you can get it back through God's grace.

Never stress over the material things in life because when they are settled and done with, you can't take them to the grave. All the money, cars, houses, females, and clothes are only satisfying for the flesh to lust for.

Remember... everybody you used to look down on when you were riding that high horse, they'll still be around. Ask them for help when everything disappears, and you are back at the bottom. They will still lend you a helping hand just to show you something.

A life lesson well learned from surrounding yourself with the wrong crowd will only expose itself in a scheduled rhythm. But the ones that still help are the ones you used to make fun of for barely making it through life.

Poverty and misfortune bring the best out of us. When we feel like our hands and feet are no longer helpful. We start using our heads, discovering the forces of the brain, trying to figure out how to turn negative into positive. Obstacles come with the challenges of the struggle; what you do with the opportunities to form new habits is up to you when you're ready to advance. Don't rush anything; work on patience. Once you fail, all it means is to reconstruct and re-strategize your plans for a better outcome. Worrying about fleshly equipment is only for the fools. Focus more on the spiritual aspect with applied faith. Operate motions to aid your desired purpose in succeeding. Success is the best revenge; retaliation from pain only causes more pain to reoccur.

Upon the situation, it's a back-and-forth, never-ending, devilish cycle taught to us at an early age. Manipulation is easily served to the unknown, so they take advantage of the non-experienced. Mostly, the younger generation has no clue what they want out of life yet. The youth is a target of the demonic. In the same way, humans break, train, and subdue animals, and they do the same to lower intelligence.

Chapter 3

We, the people, need to stop being greedy with our wisdom, knowledge, and understanding. When we see the younger ones experiencing trouble from what we know the answer to. We, the people, need to help build each other up instead of kicking each other down while on the ground. Help them get up and demonstrate a different route. Being a witness to somebody's weakness should encourage you to patch up the damaged bridge so the next group of people and you can move forward safely. Make sure your techniques are reusable. Two minds are better than one; for example, you get more power out of two batteries rather than one. The more, the better.

Tony Aldana

They know if we, the people, come together and unite as one, we become a powerful and unstoppable force, so what's the most innovative way to overcome a more powerful force by outsmarting us? Separating us into categories brings confusion; confusion unfolds arguments, arguments lead to disagreements, and disagreements cause war between the people. Some people may be physically grown, but mentally, physically, and spiritually, we need to grow up. The label of aging penetrated our minds, how we are supposed to look a certain way as we age. We, the people, need to realize we are like wine. I believe we will become better and stronger in due time. We, the people, need to stop limiting each other because some people can't meet our expectations. So we're quick to judge each other, who makes more money, whose house is bigger, whose car looks fancier, who wears regular clothes, if you don't wear designer clothes, you're not important because your money is looking funny, but it's all a lie. The list goes on and on; they puncture our minds with fear, which paralyzes us from using our full potential from thoughts independently as a functioning muscle.

We, the people, must be accurate thinkers to break the curse of being hypnotized by them. Reading books helps us expand our decision-making process, making our consideration more direct. We, the people, need to care more about each other until the shoe is on the other foot and something bad happens to someone close by. That's when empathy sets in. While strangers get brushed off, people turn the other way when it's help calling from the community. We, the people in the slums, are careless and selfish because of the poor circumstances we grew up in, which molded us to trust no one, especially in the streets. We lived by the rules and regulations of the codes that made us believe in their structure and discipline, but it's actually a trap. It's a recipe made for disaster. Tragedies destroy everything, including peace, love, and faith. Somebody lied to us, the people, to show love towards something so much that we can't see the truth behind the mask that was plotting and scheming, using manipulation to satisfy other demons.

Deception was programmed for others to take credit for what the adolescent does on the battlefields of the streets. Devious maneuvers for falsifying personal gain only activate mischievous actions toward the unseasonal minors. Making them feel like they owe something, so they catch a body for somebody. But that somebody doesn't show the same devotion when the time presents itself. We, the people, were made to shine like a bag full of diamonds. Our last mistake is our best influencer.

The younger generation is easily controlled by anything and everything because father figures, older brothers, cousins, and family members are either dead or locked up for a very long time. They feel that since the proper guidance was missing in action, they don't have to concentrate on counseling from the experienced troops. It's the blind leading the blind. There's nobody to blame but ourselves.

To become a teacher, you have to be a leader. To become a leader, you have to be a teacher.

Just because you went to college to be an instructor doesn't mean the ghetto children will listen to you.

They feel there is no understanding since you didn't go through the struggle together. How can you explain the feeling of hunger and pain when you were born with a silver spoon in your mouth? I was born with a plastic spoon in my mouth. Students model after other students; every teacher was a student at one time. To reach the observer of the lesson so they can study, students have to pay attention to the instructor's instructions. We, the people, demand respect back. The first thing little children do is fight to get their point across, but grown people need to understand the circumstances before they turn into a problem that can't be avoided. We, the people of God, stand firm with confidence that the Lord above will lead the way.

Chapter 4

Females are godly creations, perfect sculptures chiseled just for men. Never worship them, but do feel free to spoil them only when the time is appropriate. Females are the only living faculty able to form another life inside, with the remnant of a male. Mothers, aunts, ladies, madams, cousins, and sisters stop teaching little girls and inexperienced girls that the fastest way to receive anything is by what's between their legs. Rushing immature body parts can force unlawful acts from unfair crowds.

A special method is needed to assist our females in falling victim to what the media has shown them. Using music to make them think it's okay to slow dance in a sexual motion, half-naked, is the only proper way to grasp the attention of an audience. Adults' actions will blend the younger females into confusion.

Thoughts of dizziness will alter the choices to seem right when things go wrong. A lot of females are smarter and brighter than males. They lower their standards to make the relationship work. Some of their actions will hurt their partners' feelings, so they take it to the grave. They tell you what you want to hear in the form of puzzles and clues. Nobody wants a commitment with someone who is entitled to slow reactions because it will dull the relationship. Many of us "males" get our best perception of females from females. Whether it's from our mothers, aunts, cousins, sisters, or girlfriends. We run circles around each other. Love is a powerful four-letter word. Don't misuse it if you don't mean it. Words paint pictures; don't say it just to get what you want; words can blind people's judgment from the facts of the truth.

Females are the backbone of males. Look at every successful person in the world; they have an inspiring other half standing next to them. Females drive males to push harder towards achieving whatever they want in life. Together, we built a castle from the ground up. Built to last through any stormy weather approaching as a threat. The solution of an equation is discussed between the couple before they reach an agreement making a decision together. Not all females are the same.

Some are more emotional than others. Some are independent Boss females. Some are more truthful and loyal than the people you grew up with. Some are habitual liars for no reason; they love to lie. Some can't function without a male; they would rather be nurtured by a male.

I need you as you need me. We need each other. Without me, there is no you. Without you, there's no me. We need each other, we are a team now, smile, there is somebody for everybody. Where one hurts you, the next one will pleasure you; where one broke your heart, the next person will patch it up. Where one hits you, the next individual will kiss you.

Females will earn their position based on what they want to be labeled as. Every female wants to be a queen but doesn't meet the expectations to be labeled one. An angry female is your worst enemy.

The girlfriend knows you like the back of your hand. Their actions spit venom just like their mouths drip honey. Their words can rip hearts apart. A female with a monstrous heart and wicked soul will destroy you instead of improving you. But a female with virtuous values and morals will help you sprout.

They must be treated like a trophy placed on top, well-protected from damage, and kept away from dirt. I appreciate the ladies for preserving our population from extinction. Reasonable protocols should be a performance willing to bring forward to the younger females at an early age to find themselves before the perverted stalk them like prey. Keep them in activities so they stay busy with no room for curiosity, and make them concentrate on their future first. To find their hidden talents, keep them doing different activities like sports, band instruments, arts, cooking, and designing, things to find the giant within.

Females are natural providers; it's in their DNA; it is embedded in them to care for and provide for a child since birth. For example, when a baby is crying, we, the males, make a bottle without thinking twice. Then, the child's mother will say, "No, go warm it up first, but not too hot." She'll say,

"Check it before you give it to the baby." The baby is still crying, so we try to rock the baby to sleep, but we still have no success.

Now, ask the mother again what seems to be the problem before we return the baby back to her. She'll look at the baby and say she or he is hot and take the baby's clothes off. If it ain't no diaper change, it's just the newborn's way of letting us know something is wrong. Since they can't communicate through words, they talk by crying. Take all the babies clothes off and leave them in a diaper. Now watch the baby just look at you and start smiling with sinless eyes.

Never let your brother, uncle, cousin, nephew, or next-door neighbor place your little girl on his lap, acting like she is riding a horse and he is shaking his leg really fast up and down. That thing between a female's legs, old or young, is highly sensitive. It will send mixed signals to the little girl at an early age. That improper conduct contaminated her mind way too early.

Chapter 5

Do you know what a wolf in sheep's clothing is? A wolf can't approach a crowd or herd of prey without getting scared, nervous, and panicking, so they scatter and run away to live to see another day. A smart wolf will catch one sheep, skin it, and wear the fur as a disguise to hide his identity as he hunts again. The wolf can protect and provide for its family without the pack. The wolf has a lion's courage and a gorilla's heart. Now the real question is, are you a wolf or prey? A lot of people pray for the best but expect the worst.

It doesn't make sense to me to pray for the best, which you will never witness, because your expectations are drowned by doubt and fear. Placing restrictions around yourself is self-demolishing to your beliefs. Falling victim to the system's program is easy to do and hard to come out of. The blueprint is for us to depend on them. For example, when we came to prison, they provided us with state clothes and shoes, fed us three times a day, and gave us shelter with a roof over our heads.

So when it rains, we dry; when it's cold, they give us jackets to keep us warm. It is similar to the food stamps, S.S.I. checks, and section "A" apartments available to the community. They institutionalized the brain; the body follows once you control the mind. After being caged for so many years and finally released back into society, there is no adjustment. So, a return to a penal institution is granted by the state.

They say knowledge is power, but it's just stored memory. Just because you read a book about making money does not mean you're going to be a millionaire. Or just because you read the bible and go to church every Sunday doesn't mean you are saved. As soon as you finish reading the bible or come back from church, you do the opposite of what the Father is teaching us. It's Basic. Instruction. Before. Leaving. Earth.

Once you apply the information, the power sets in from the books you read and studied. Put it into action; that's the only way the power unfolds from the facts of a subject. Putting it into practice with a particular use is necessary. If you ever look into the ocean, the water looks blue, but the water is so clear that it's the reflection of the sky because if you dip a cup in the water, it's clear. I can make a middle school student present himself as a college student by reading the dictionary.

Every night for two hours to raise a more desirable speech-compatible person that's agreeable to all because we live in a judgmental world where the way we speak will set us in a defined division of classification from the words that we choose. People will form opinions about others from the way they talk. How they walk, and why they look different, but correct me if I'm wrong. But God never created anyone who has, have, or had an identical fingerprint. People's assumptions shouldn't affect you because they only Judge with their eyes. But who's to say their eyes are correct and your eyes are wrong?

We are naturally competitive specimens. When we see someone performing a task to completion, it motivates us to want to accomplish a task to completion. For example, when working out and exercising with a partner and he or she is working out hard, it makes us want to work out harder. However, someone who envies others will only take away and give nothing in return, for example, when someone walks into a room with a sexy female standing next to him. The first thing a hater thinks about is what he can do to sleep with her behind his back instead of having a constructive competitive attitude and finding a better-looking female who's more exclusive than beautiful than her. Iron sharpens iron, compete in a positive manner, and never compare yourself to the next person. Humble yourself. You have to love yourself first and foremost. How are you going to love someone else if you don't even love yourself? You are just damaging yourself. Train yourself for excellence; don't beg for anything. Demand it out of life.

There's a difference between being a young, foolish person and being an old, foolish person. A young, foolish person is still learning in the journey of life. Hence, they still have time to correct themselves because they don't know, but when you are old and foolish, there is no fixing them because you are stuck in your old ways, and you will never be able to show an old dog new tricks if it doesn't want to learn. Worrying about the next person and what they've got going on is bad news; it's only right that you move on to your own path.

Chapter 6

Family is forever like diamonds, and the rest is temporary. Many people will come in and out of your life, but family ain't going nowhere. We're connected like cement. Never turn your back on family; if a fallout presents itself, let the emotions fade away and be the mature one to pull back up for reinforcement.

Not all family members are favorable to you; learn the difference between who's who. Some family members will only give you something to receive something back in return. Some family members will provide you with anything out of the kindness of their heart without wanting anything in return.

They say blood is thicker than water, but you need water in your life so the blood won't dry up because it's too thick. Some family members will treat you like a total stranger. So, the water is family, not related by blood, but the family is related by loyalty.

A family tree should be made to inform the new members of the family's history and come together to form an astonishing book for the next generation to read, study, and learn. Add new branches to the family tree, and the old leaves regenerate to take over. Take care of your tree to keep it healthy and everything intact. God will water it to keep it growing. I used to be ruthless, dismantling everything and anything I came in contact with. A couple of family members gave up on me, but the ones who believed in me outweighed the rest.

I see the bigger picture now: family gets tired of watching each other make the same errors, so they allow us to keep hurting ourselves until we are ready to stop inflicting harm on ourselves. We injure their feelings, too, and our reputation. We can't keep doing the same thing and expect different results to appear; that's called insanity. Replace the formula with a more suitable response.

The family will go to the fullest extent for each other when the moment is necessary, and no questions will be asked. Family members are the front line for one another. Cousins will step up to the plate, taking the position of brothers and uncles, and will consolidate nephews, making them mentally, physically, and spiritually stronger to secure them from the vultures. Family will test each other to see where they stand with one another, to make somebody vanish quickly, let them borrow some money. The ones that respect your values will pay you back and keep associating with you. But the ones that are just around you to drain your electricity will never come back for the simple fact that they owe you.

Money is the root of all evil; money doesn't have emotions; it's the people who cherish the money that put feelings behind the piece of paper. Money will cut through flesh like butter; it burns relationships into ashes.

To be the head, not the tail, the family will only listen to transmitted data if displayed confidently, bringing everybody together for family events or ceremonies. Make every family member feel comfortable with each other so no information is held back from the younger ones. We are supposed to be the band-aid to the wounded, to contribute to the effect of improvement. Growing up with a big family, they had a lot of friends, so when they threw parties, they were packed with older people and children everywhere.

Some family and some friends were familiar with each other growing up. So our family even seemed bigger. As time went by, this changed, and so did people. One of my uncles went to prison for murder when I was a kid. It was me, my mom, and grandma standing in the kitchen. I remember my uncle running inside the house with blood on his clothes, saying he just shot his close friend by accident when my uncle was explaining everything to my grandma and my mom.

I was just looking at the blood on his shirt. My uncle said he was going to kill himself because he loved and cared for his best friend.

My uncle ran out of the house to a church close by, where the cops finally found him. Since it was a "22" cal. The bullet bounced around his friend's body. So he wasn't pronounced dead until hours later. They gave my uncle 15 years in T.D.C.J. My mom, my grandma, and I visited my uncle more than anybody else.

Faithfully, we were there. My uncle came home a couple of years ago. The family circle became smaller ever since those hazardous events occurred, but the ones with absolute attachment are still around. The fewer people around you, the better because you can concentrate with greater advantage without the fog. When the smoke clears, your comprehension of circumstances is more visual because family is divine.

Tony Aldana

Chapter 7

Brothers, our word is bond. If your word ain't shit, you ain't shit. I am my brother's keeper, so I must install the regulations for a movement of purpose with all my brothers. We honor each other so we can contribute to the advancement of sharpening our minds to the extreme with a lifetime scholarship to teach a whole nation. My brothers and I came a long way from wet dirt, so it is mandatory that we glisten together to distinguish us from a mile away because our halos are bright out of this world. Bringing light into the darkness. Were community representatives manufacturing in progress for change within ourselves and our surroundings? My brothers and I were born conductors and organized generals, and we have never been to Hollywood. So, doing things for fame is not in us. Me and my brothers are labeled as ghetto celebrities without making movies. My brothers and I know where we came from; now, we know the differences of what we don't want to return to. Let sideline comments from fans stay on the sideline.

While my brothers and I played the game, we let cheer leaders cheer, and commentators comment. Eventually, I became the coach that set plays up for our all-star team. We have motion together. Displaying talents that got the world's considerations ratified, proceed climbing the ladder. Become the owner, watching everything from binoculars inside the sky box. Me and my brothers dictate our own emotions being attached to us. My brothers and I are not puppets cutting all strings of emotions that are being pulled by others who want us to perform how they want us to. Controlled emotions win every time, cracking the code without a cheat sheet. How can you argue with someone who's laughing at your stupidity by smiling in your face? You're just arguing with yourself. The other person has no response.

Don't let other people have control over you from your own emotions. Master your own feelings before someone else will. Me and my brothers lead by example. I can't stand to see any of my brothers doing poorly in my presence. If their shoes or shirts are dirty, I will come off the shirt, leaving me shirtless or shoeless for my brothers' type of love I demonstrate. You can feel it in your heart when you do something righteous, just like you hear it before you do anything wrong. We starved together, so it's only right we get full together, and there are no empty stomachs in our circles. Nobody gets left behind when the movement is forward. Good vibes are left in the atmosphere; don't surround yourself with people who practice the wrong, corrupted lifestyle, and stay content with failure "elevate."

Be careful who you associate with; eagles soar with eagles, vultures crum with vultures. To catch both of them flying together is impossible. Whatever the eagle can't finish devouring its food, it leaves the leftovers to the vultures. Me and Lil' Eastside are the only two brothers out of the four of us who have been to prison. Even though I was living with no major purpose but selling drugs to survive in the jungle, the fast money had me blinded, feeling soulless at times, possessed by those street life demons. My brothers are all I had left even when everybody turned its back on us. I have seen my youngest brother, black , who looks up to me, influenced by the hustling late at night. Thugging with my comrades on our block, The "U-Turn," AKA The "ZOO-Turn." I remember telling black one night to go home, this ain't no live shit. What are we doing? I know it looks all good and lavish right now, but it ain't; I have been locked up your whole life, little bro, and what comes with this lifestyle is separation from loved ones. He looked disappointed, but I was telling him for his better. I told him it's bad enough that me and little Eastside been fucking up, and you decided to do the same; we are going to kill Momma faster.

I'm grateful he listened to me because, until this day, my little brother, black and chikis, graduated. Out of all four of us, now Lil' Eastside did a major shift that blew my mind. He went from going to T.D.C.J. twice to bouncing back into a legally self-made Boss as he told me he was out of state getting money.

Chapter 8

A mother's love is unconditional when it comes to her children, leaving the world speechless if they only knew the truth. She's a custodian of our feelings and a personal angel in our lives. Many people haven't witnessed this miracle, so we cherish it with everything we have. Love your Momma to the point you'll always protect her. Don't be too open with telling them everything because we kill our own parents unintentionally. Only tell them the good parts, even if everything is all bad momentarily. Worries turn into stress, stress builds up depression, and depression transpires into disease's cause of death. I know you and Momma have an electrified relationship of friends, but realize, you're still Momma's little baby at the end of the day. Don't take advantage of Momma; we don't know how good something was until it's gone. Nobody lives forever, so a photograph of Momma's face or a special moment should be stored in our minds. We have to know the difference between Momma and our wives. There are two different people. Both of them are our queens, but we never compare them because Momma is Momma, and wifey is wifey. Momma's stay cautious when newborn infants are in the same bed. Especially when sleeping together. I know you want the baby by your side at all times. But when it's time to sleep at night, please have a cradle nearby so you can attend to the baby's needs when they do cry. Remember, a newborn can't talk to warn you, only cries, hoping you understand. You can't sleep with a newborn baby in the same way because accidents can occur. We move a lot as adults when we sleep, so imagine you smooshing the little one or the covers suffocating the sinless. It's better to be safe than sorry. Flowers should be personally delivered to all your loved ones still living. Momma should be up there on top of the list with wifey. What good is it if you can't see their facial expressions when these special gifts are giving? It feels good to make them smile. Why wait till they are in a grave to bring them flowers? That is selfish behavior, showing them affection while they are still breathing and showing them that they are appreciated. Recognize the quality of affection given to us from being 9 months inside of Momma's stomach to being brought into a world of mostly evil. She made us feel lavish even though we were broken. She kept us safe from harm as children. Informed us to stay aware of the emotionally violent female tornado and how to separate the difference between GOOD and BAD females no matter the final decision from the conclusion reached after consideration. Momma will ride with you, right or wrong. She will be by your side, just a phone call away.

Mothers have to be alert of negativity around babies because always thinking negatively about the baby will rub off. Thinking about the little ones being sick with colds will eventually cause the innocent to become sick from bad thoughts planted by their mother. To be attentive is to be alive. Always have positive thoughts about babies; they are well protected by the one and only Father, "ALLAH." I'm grateful for my Big Queen Grandma and King Grandpa for bringing my beautiful mother, the Queen of all Queens in this world. One day, I was asleep at my grandma's house in my uncle's room. "He was incarcerated at the time. But my grandma woke me up from a deep sleep early in the morning. At the moment, I was thugging, hustling hard, just another victim of the system. A lost soul to the game. The undercovers raided my aunt's house directly in front of the window. I could see white trucks and SUVs everywhere, and then my big cousin came out of the house in handcuffs.

I have never seen him go to jail. When my grandma woke me up, she told me to give her everything I got. So she can hide my contraband. So I did what she said as soon as they left, and the coast was clear. She gave me everything back. My grandma has old timers where she forgets a lot of places or things but not people. I know she doesn't remember everything, but I do, and she will live through me and you forever. God bless my grandmas and yours for having a big, courageous heart. I see where my mom gets it from. She always stood by my side through the whole thunderstorm while everybody else ran for cover to protect themselves. When I come home, it's time to show my momma how much I really appreciate her for everything she's done for me. From mine to yours, always keep an intense feeling of deep affection that will never disappear. I love you, Momma.

Chapter 9

A wizard is like quicksand. Don't try to walk over it unless you want to sink into the dirt. Voodoo is jumbo mumbo for the brain cells. Once you allow superstitious beliefs to exploit within, is how your holy temple crumbles. Bring life to the cemetery. People can be half dead cherishing the hopeless. Bring light to their chambers. We have powers of the conscious, and then you have the positive, inspiring voices from a higher power. While evil, destructive, wicked voices from the coward himself. You can tell the difference of voices; God's voice is calm and peaceful, his words are clear, and his voice sends chills down your spine. Tears automatically fall down your cheeks, while the other voices are so negative.

Evil will distance the blessings deserved. It's been written down in stone from day one: the one and only creator gives extra strength, mentally and spiritually; God boosts the extra energy to a climax times×2 for the joy of life. Your subconscious gives you the "Right of control," which means that you can control it, it does not mean that you do control it. You must learn to exercise this right as a matter of habit through any dominating idea, plan, or purpose held in your conscious. Acting upon through repeated effort and emotionalized by a burning desire. For its realization is taken over by the subconscious, acting through any natural and logical means may be available. The conscious mind is where reasoning and thinking occur. It analyzes information and data; it acts as a guardian of the doorway of the subconscious. The conscious mind develops as a result of experiences. The subconscious mind doesn't think, reason, or deliberate. The subconscious can be compared with a car.

At the same time, the conscious mind can be considered the driver. The power is in the car, not the driver. The diver must learn to release and direct the power. The subconscious mind receives any image that is transferred to it by the conscious mind under strong emotions. No matter how solid we form ourselves from emotions, emotions may fade away but always re-appear. It's the way God made us; all positive emotions are good, so just accept it. From the temples of Egypt and Mexico, two different places in the world. The temples are so perfectly aligned, and they are all built the same way in different places in the world. It could have been the help and assistance of something extra. If you pay attention to the drawings on the walls inside the pyramids, they are all pointing up at a higher power with a plan.

By adding water to make the rocks that weighed tons now weigh as light as a feather. It's up to you to believe how these beautiful temples were built. When we age and move daily, we develop blood clots in places like legs, arms, back, feet, etc. The solution to the problem is whole pickles with pickle juice. You instantly feel the relief of your heart complies by enhancing its paste in heartbeats. If you're not a pickle fan, just try onions or garlic. Either way, it's really good for your body health. Wise, remember we don't live forever anyway.

Back in the bible days, people lived 100 years, but now, people are blessed to even live to see 50, 60, or 80. You must be detailed about what you will give before you expect to get it in return. No one gets anything for nothing. People with currency to give will expect to receive something in return: A product, a service, or an increase in their capital.

You won't be successful overnight. In fact, you won't be successful until you have returned to everyone who aided you with everything that he or she is due. Extraordinarily disciplined minds are well needed; don't just nod your head in agreement with this. Know your strengths and weaknesses.

A structure made from the ground up will make any foundation solid enough to stand up against any storm. There are numerous examples of this power. Christ himself allied with his disciples to carry out his work. The plan was his own, but it survived betrayal and his absence to achieve success beyond human comprehension.

Make sure your first introduction is your best introduction. People will only remember you from the first time of agreement of presentation from the meeting at hand. People will feel unappreciated if you don't remember them, even if you have to go along with it until the memory catches up. If possible, it's a code of honor.

Chapter 10

I'm a habitual convicted felon, mostly for selling drugs. I was facing 25-years, but they said they could get me 16 years. I wondered if they went from 25 to 16 years in 15 to 20 minutes. I know I can talk them down to sign at a lower time. I shot a number out there close to the years I'll be willing to sign today to go do my time and come home. I ended up doing 5 years. My T.D.C.J. transfer facility was the holiday unit in Huntsville, TX. I got G-4 off that unit in a month, and now I'm headed to the Smith Unit. We did a pit stop at French Robertson in Abilene, TX. My celly at that pit stop was from Dallas, TX. He ended up having a tattoo gun, so he inked my neck up. Once I got to Smith Unit in Lamesa, TX.

I figured out it's a rascal unit where it's 90% youngin's. So, it's always turned up. In a month, I got a G5 for popping out the cell. So now they send me to the "ISLAND," which is the high-security side of the unit. Lockdown 23 hours out of the day. One time, they opened all the cell doors in one row. Only certain people came out thugging. Then, two-row cell doors opened. A riot unfolded in the blink of an eye. Long story short, they shipped everybody on an emergency chain to McConnell Unit in Beeville, TX. When you are a G-5, you don't have an assigned unit. You are at the bottom of the barrel. At McConnell Unit, G-5 was too turned up. The youngins started a fire because the commissary lady left. In a month, they separated everyone who came from the Smith Unit. I ended up in Livingston, TX, Polunsky Unit G-5. Let me remind you: G-5 holds all the troublemakers around TX. Then, in Polunsky's "TL" Unit, separated from the rest of the

Unit, they hold "Death Row." I lasted a year. They G-4 me to Clemens Unit in Brazoria County, TX, which was another rascal unit full of young people. I lasted about a month G-5 to Hughes Unit Gatesville, TX. This unit was like no other unit I have ever been in. Got there, G-5.

Once I made it to G-4, everything changed in my life towards elevating my way of thinking from what I learned in the streets. My mind was open now, and I was attracted to progress. It wasn't easy because being accustomed to change was not normal. From riots, lineups, and 23-hour lockdowns to a little bit more freedom in G-4.

Same stuff, different scenario; this time, I turned the TV off. Being TANGO BLAST from H-Town but far away from the city. You really are in somebody else's backyard. So it's a little city plex in the air when outnumbered, but it's still all Good. So, one day, I got disciplined after I slapped and almost put him to sleep from the slap. So I fought that one person for 3 to 4 rounds till he ran out of breath. He didn't want to fight anymore after the air ran out of his lungs. As soon as I finished catching my breath, the discipline occurred.

I fought 2 HBs for about three rounds. I came out looking good, but I had a little bump on the side of my ear. I got dropped twice but got back on my feet faster than you can blink. I was even dropping them, too. I was mad for a while, so I told some HBs I wanted to go solo and fight every HB one-on-one, which disciplined me. "LMAO." As soon as I told him that, he said go put your shoes on. That's another two-on-one. Let me remind you: I was the only Houston HB on that pod. I put my shoes on. As a man, I was tired of bullshit from them playing the favoritism game and choosing sides without knowing the truth. So, I left Tango Blast alone; I only talked to the HBs I knew were stomped down from other Units. The love was still there, but things were different then. It wasn't the same as when I first blasted in 07. It was just a penitentiary thing, but now I'm tired of this penitentiary. That's when I started fighting every day.

Got hit one day with a fan motor, but he didn't hit me right because it felt just like a punch, so I got up off my seat in the day room. I tried to run up on him, but he kept swinging the fan motor in a sox. They made the dude put the weapon down and fight me one-on-one. I shined that day I put on for the city because I slept him, woke him up, slept him again while he was still on the ground, and then walked off. I ended up fighting my celly, and that's how I ended up with another battle scar on top of my head because my celly pushed me. He felt the pressure, and it seemed like they would only fight me when I would take "drills."

Those pills are the closest to being dranked out. Sober me is a different story; I didn't have any problems. So the HBs told me I gotta go because I had been tripping. I just got into a fight with another HB after lunch. I told them you gotta kill me because I ain't going nowhere. They surrounded me, but the "Ol Skool" HB from West TX with a life sentence said we needed more HBs like you and shook my hand. The store was in a couple of days, so he hooked me up with some cookies and soups. Long story short, nothing changed until I wanted to change, and I got tired of getting the same results.

God is always with us even when we think he's not. He's looking and listening. He tried to open my eyes early, but I didn't want to change them back then. I wasn't ready, trapped in those streets. Even after I became blind from my right eye, I couldn't see the truth. God wanted me to still live for his reason, not mine. I didn't know my purpose and became worse than I was at first. It was me and three other homies from the hood.

We went to this female's house, but two other people from a different neighborhood were already there. An argument broke out. So the females told us to go in the house, but we didn't know they were at a party at a couple of houses down the same street. We were young, and they were way older. I was under the influence of Xanax, so I wasn't thinking correctly. I wasn't in my right state of mind. I remember being with E inside the house in the kitchen; I had some Hennessey and a couple of Xanax pills. I gave him some and popped some more.

After that, my memory faded away. A couple of months later, I woke up in the hospital, clueless about why I was there. I remember seeing family members all around me. It's like I'm still high, so I go back to sleep in a coma. While I was asleep, it was like I was still running the streets in my hood off Federal Road. Right before I finally woke up, someone grabbed me and put me back in my physical body. "Now I know it was a god" because I woke up in the hospital bed for good. My mom told me the doctor asked her if she wanted to disconnect the breathing tube. I had a breathing tube breathing for me for a month or two; I tried to speak, but they couldn't hear me. They were so happy to see me alive, and it was a happy moment for all of us. The doctors came in, so I tried to leave. As soon as I got up, they sat me back down. And told me I could go if I walked out the door.

If not, I have to stay for therapy as soon as I take my first step. I failed, but they caught me before I touched the ground. My skull has cracks in it, so it messed up my right vision. The veins in my eye pop, it's clogged up, and blood dried up, so my vision died out that eyeball, leaving me with no pulpal.

Years later, I'm still in and out of prison with no direction, but this time down, God touched me spiritually. One night, after me and my celly were chopping it up, he asked me, if God asked you to jump off a cliff, would you do it, "he said he got, u don't worry about nothing. I thought about it long and hard for 3 minutes, then I said yea, my celly told me he didn't know what he would say; it's a tricky question when it comes to trust. I prayed before I went to sleep, but when I finished praying this time, my tongue tasted like Sprite, a cold cup of Sprite mixed with big red for a couple of seconds. It was so real it spooked me. As soon as I got up to tell my celly the watch on my wrist fell off. I looked at it for a couple of seconds, then told my celly what I had experienced and my tears of joy. Just started falling off my face. I didn't even bother to wipe them away. He started tearing up, too.

My celly negro has been gone 20 years plus. That night, I prayed again. I told God he got me; I'll do whatever he wants me to do. I asked him to show me again that it was real. I looked around expecting something to fall or move, and nothing happened, but as soon as I closed my eyes to lie down. I felt a thump on my back under the metal of the locker to my bunk. I got goosebumps but couldn't get scared because God is love and peace. He will never harm you. Even when it is judgment day, he will punish you by sending you on the way to get tortured by the opposite of him. My faith is stronger than ever. I still pray by putting my all into it, including my soul. I got a lay-in for the legal mail room two days later, so I didn't understand it. So, I had someone explain it to me better who understood better on the legal part. He told me that the Houston Forensic Science Center hired this lady here. She was fired because she was doing some illegal stuff under their noses. So, as soon as I get out, I need a lawyer to represent me because my case falls under her. Trust and believe in God; he will give you the world and everything in it. That same night, I dreamed that I had two pupils.

www.ingramcontent.com/pod-product-compliance
Lightning Source LLC
LaVergne TN
LVHW051036070526
838201LV00010B/224